The Ladybird Book of

KINGS & QUEENS OF ENGLAND

The Ladybird Book of

KINGS & QUEENS OF ENGLAND

Written by Louise Jones
Illustrated by Robin Davies and John Dillow
Front cover and crown on back cover illustrated by Nick Hardcastle
Portraits illustrated by Jon Jackson

871 – 1485

1485 – Present Day

The Ladybird Book of

KINGS & QUEENS
OF ENGLAND

Part 1
871 – 1485

The Kingdoms of Saxon Britain

Offa's Dyke

In the 8th century, Offa, the Saxon king of Mercia (who called himself 'King of the English'), drove the Celts into Wales. He built an earthen wall 240 kilometres (150 miles) long, with a ditch to keep them there. The Welsh word for the English, 'seis', like the Scottish 'sassenach', really means 'Saxon'.

Britain Before Alfred

In the centuries before the arrival of the Romans, Britain was not ruled as one nation, but was divided among many separate tribes, who lived in the forests that covered most of the land. The Celtic tribes of Britain chose their kings (or chieftains) by election. If a king did not act fairly and look after his people, he was **deposed** and replaced by a new king.

The Romans ruled Britain between 43 and 410. Celtic rule was restored after the Romans left, but by then many Celts were Christian. Towards the end of the Roman period, invaders from Germany and Denmark (Saxons, Angles and Jutes) attacked the east coast of Britain.

The Saxons (as all these invaders became known) settled in Britain, and occupied southern England. They drove the Celts back to the far north (Scotland) and west (Wales and Cornwall). Then, the Saxons divided England into kingdoms. At different times, powerful kings of particular kingdoms ruled the whole country.

From the 790s onwards, Viking raiders came from Scandinavia in longships: killing, **plundering** and taking slaves. In around 860 the Vikings formed an army to conquer Britain, and took possession of large areas of England. By 870 only the Saxon kingdom of **Wessex** remained unconquered. Wessex, under a great Saxon leader, Alfred, held out against the Viking invaders.

Viking invaders
The Saxons had been violent in their invasions. The Vikings were even more violent.

Arthur in battle
Early historians tell of a great Celtic leader called Arthur. He defeated the Saxons many times in the 6th century.

BEFORE ALFRED

ALFRED THE GREAT
871-899 (b. 849)

The 'Alfred' jewel

This gold and enamel jewel has the inscription: 'Alfred ordered me to be made'.
It is probably the head of a bone or ivory pointer, used to point to words when reading. Alfred sent out pointers with his newly-translated books.

Alfred The Great

Alfred was the youngest of the five warri or sons of Ethelwulf, the Saxon King of Wessex. In 870 he proved himself a great warrior, fighting the Danes. Because of this, in 871 the people chose him as king. That year Alfred fought the Danish invaders nine times. He fortified the kingdom of Wessex, formed a navy, and organised his army so that half guarded the kingdom while the other half farmed.

In 877 the Danes attacked Alfred's palace at Chippenham, Wiltshire, and he fled to the Athelney marshes in Somerset. The following year, Alfred broke out of hiding and retook his palace at the Battle of Edington, Wiltshire. He made peace with the Danes and agreed that they should rule East Anglia, while he could concentrate on ruling southern England.

Guthrum, the Danish leader, took Christian baptism, and Alfred was his sponsor.

In 885 Alfred invited Asser, a great Celtic scholar and priest, to work for him. Asser taught Alfred Latin and helped him to devise a system of just laws. Alfred became a learned king and won the respect of the Celts. He had great books translated into **Anglo-Saxon**, and he founded schools. His chief law was, 'Do not do to others what you would not want done to you.' Alfred is the only English monarch to be called 'The Great'.

Alfred and Asser
Alfred employed the Celtic scholar Asser as his teacher and adviser, and won the respect of the Celts.

A burh
Alfred built many fortified towns, called 'burhs', to defend his kingdom. Deep ditches and banks of earth were set round them.

EDWARD (the Elder)
899-924 (b. 870)
ATHELSTAN
924-939 (b. 895)
EDMUND
(the Magnificent)
939-946 (b. 920)
EDRED *946-955*
(b. 923)
EDWY *955-959*
(b. 941)

Ethelfleda
in battle
*From 917 to 918
Edward's sister
Ethelfleda, Queen
of Mercia, led her
forces into battle
in his support.
By 918, when
Ethelfleda died, she
and Edward ruled
most of England.*

Alfred's Family

Alfred's son, Edward the Elder, spent most of his reign fighting to push back the **frontiers** of the **Danelaw** (the Viking part of England).

Edward's eldest son, King Athelstan, was a hero who fought Vikings and Celts. He formed England into roughly the area it occupies today. Athelstan was the first of his family who could read and write from childhood. He was **devout**, and he drew up good laws.

In 937 Athelstan defeated a combined Danish and Celtic force at the Battle of Brunanburh, north Yorkshire.

Athelstan was the most powerful British ruler since the Romans, and he brought peace and unity.

Many foreign kings sent him gifts, and poets came to sing his praises.

Athelstan's brothers, Edmund and Edred, spent their reigns strengthening the gains Athelstan had made. Edwy, Edmund's teenage son, was foolish and irresponsible. He is best remembered for banishing the wise Dunstan, Abbot of Glastonbury. This was because when Edwy left his coronation feast to visit his fiancée, Dunstan tried to persuade him to return. Edwy was eventually forced off the throne by the rulers of Mercia and Northumberland.

Athelstan receiving a foreign ambassador
He was the first Anglo-Saxon king to rule the whole of England. He was known and admired throughout the Christian world. Foreign rulers sent him gifts, and asked his permission to take his sisters as their wives.

A coin of Athelstan's reign
He passed the first English laws controlling the issue of coinage, with severe penalties for **counterfeiters**.

EDGAR
(the Peaceful)
959-975 (b. 942)
EDWARD
(the Martyr)
975-978 (b. 962)
ETHELRED II
(the Unready)
978-1013, 1014-1016
(b. 968)
SWEYN (Forkbeard)
1013-1014 (b. 960)

Six sub-kings (mostly Celts) pay tribute to Edgar's power by rowing him across the River Dee

This was in 973, the year he was crowned 'King of the Anglo-Saxon Empire'.

Saxons and Danes

The reign of Edgar, Edwy's brother and successor, was a 'golden age'. Edgar recalled Dunstan, Abbot of Glastonbury, from exile, and made him Archbishop of Canterbury. Edgar gathered allies to help keep the peace, and was loved and honoured.

Edgar's son, Edward, was different: he was selfish and his reign was a disaster. Edward was murdered, and his 10-year-old stepbrother, Ethelred, was made king.

Ethelred did no better. He was lazy and unlucky, and useless in battle.

Danes had now become part of English society, but in 1002 Ethelred ordered that all Danes in England be killed. His order was not fully carried out; but this was an early example of racial persecution.

Ethelred's nickname, 'the Unready', was a pun on his name: 'Aethel-raed' means 'wise advice' in Anglo-Saxon; 'un-raed' means 'no advice' or 'bad advice'.

By 1011 the Danes held most of southeastern England. Ethelred paid them huge amounts of **Danegeld**, but they took more and more. In 1013 the Danish prince, Sweyn, invaded England and regained the north. Ethelred fled to Normandy, in northern France, leaving Sweyn to rule as king.

In 1014, after Sweyn died, the English asked Ethelred to return as their king. They did not want another Dane, Sweyn's son Cnut, to take the throne. Ethelred tried to punish Cnut's supporters in battle, but the attempt was a disaster and war broke out. Cnut pursued Ethelred to London to attack him. Ethelred died of natural causes, and the English accepted Cnut as king.

A comet in 975
This was seen as a bad omen for the new king Edward's reign. In 976 there was famine. This was followed by rioting and bloodshed; many monasteries were destroyed.

When a Viking force threatened the south coast of England in 1009, Ethelred told his people to pray and fast to make their enemies go away. He also had a coin minted with the Lamb of God (Jesus Christ) and the Dove (the Holy Spirit) on it, in the hope that this would help.

EDMUND (Ironside)
Apr-Nov 1016 (b. 989)
CNUT
1016-1035 (b. 995)
**HAROLD I
(Harefoot)**
1035-1040 (b. 1016)
HARTHACNUT
1040-1042 (b. 1018)

Cnut and Edmund Ironside swear brotherhood
The two agreed to govern half of the country each. Cnut took the north and Edmund took Wessex – but Edmund was dead within a month of this agreement.

Cnut and His Sons

After Ethelred died in 1016, some people wanted Edmund, his son, to become king. Others preferred Cnut. A compromise was reached, and Cnut agreed to share England with Edmund (known as Edmund Ironside because of his courage and glamour). Seven months after Ethelred's death, Edmund died, so in 1016 Cnut became king of all England. By 1030 he was king of Denmark and Norway too.

Cnut worked hard to keep hold of his lands. He was a peaceful, devoutly Christian monarch.

In 1035 Cnut died. He left two sons, Harold Harefoot and Harthacnut. They were half-brothers, and they hated each other.

Cnut meant Harthacnut to be king of England after him, but Harold took control of the country while Harthacnut was in Denmark.

Harold did not live long, and Harthacnut spent his time as king punishing the people who had helped Harold.

Harthacnut was the last of the Danish **dynasty** founded by Cnut.

Cnut and the sea

It is said that Cnut told the rising tide to stop, to show his silly, flattering courtiers that his power was far less than God's power.

After Harold's death, Harthacnut had his half-brother's body dug up and thrown into a marsh.

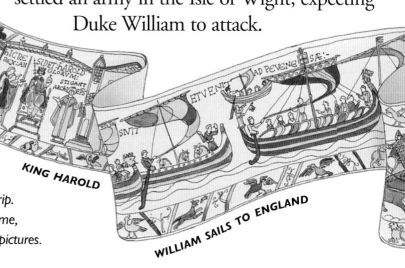

Edward and Harold II

Ethelred's son, Edward the Confessor, had a long and peaceful reign. His nickname came from his gentle manners and devotion to prayer and churchgoing.

Under the Danish kings, England had been divided among the **earls**. Wessex, home of earlier English kings, was now ruled by the powerful Earl Godwin.

Godwin died in 1053. In 1056 his son Harold went to Europe to find Edmund Ironside's son, and make him Edward's heir. But in 1057 this new heir died.

This time he told Edward's second cousin, Duke William of Normandy, that Edward wanted him to be the next king of England. But, when Edward died in 1066, he said Harold should be king.

Harold was a fine soldier: he held off an attack by Edward's exiled brother Tostig, and settled an army in the Isle of Wight, expecting Duke William to attack.

EDWARD
(the Confessor)
1042-1066 (b. 1004)
HAROLD II
(Godwinson)
Jan-Oct 1066 (b. 1020)

EDWARD'S BURIAL

KING HAROLD

WILLIAM SAILS TO ENGLAND

The Bayeux Tapestry
It was made about 1070 and tells the story of Harold and William the Conqueror, rather like a cartoon strip. Not many people could read at that time, so it was necessary to tell the story in pictures.

THE SAXONS

18

They waited, bored, for months. Soon, harvest time came and many left to gather the harvest.

William planned to sail in August, but had to wait for a favourable wind. In September, Tostig, with Harald Hardrada, King of Norway, attacked York, in the north of England. Harold rushed north and beat the invaders on 25 September, 1066 at Stamford Bridge, near York. Three days later Duke William landed near Hastings, on the south coast. Harold rode south, gathering troops as he went. William attacked before the English army was ready. The Normans were well rested and on 14 October 1066, Harold and most of his men died after fighting heroically at Senlac, near Hastings.

Ethelred's great-grandson, Edgar, was chosen king, but never crowned. William marched on London, **ravaging** the country. A party of elders met him and offered him the crown.

The 'shield wall' used by English soldiers
This made it very difficult for the enemy to wound them.

The Bayeux Tapestry is an embroidery on linen. It is 63 metres long (207 feet), and is kept in the French town of Bayeux, Normandy. It was probably made in England.

BATTLE OF HASTINGS

HAROLD'S DEATH

**WILLIAM I
(the Conqueror)**
1066-1087 (b. 1027)

**Serfs working on
their lord's land**
*William brought the
feudal system from
Normandy. Society
was divided into groups.
The lowest, the serfs,
lived on the land but
did not own it, and
were compelled to
work for their lords.*

William I

William was crowned on Christmas Day 1066, in Westminster Abbey. He strengthened Edward the Confessor's legal system, and made England into a **feudal society**. He punished rebels by taking their land, which he gave to his Norman barons. By 1085, only two of the large landowners were Anglo-Saxon.

Some Saxons did resist Norman rule. Hereward the Wake was one. He became a great Saxon hero, who led uprisings against the Normans. He was eventually outlawed and fled into hiding in the marshes of Lincolnshire, where others joined him. It is not known what happened to him, but his name became legendary.

THE NORMANS

In 1086, William listed all English land and property, with its ownership, for tax purposes. In later years his famous survey became known as 'The Domesday Book'.

William left England to his middle son, called William Rufus, who was his favourite. Robert, the eldest son, became Duke of Normandy, and Henry, the youngest, inherited a fortune. William died in France in 1087 of injuries received when his horse threw him while he was fighting the King of France. William was buried at Caen, in Normandy.

A Norman arch
The Normans brought their language and culture to England. They were descended from Vikings who had settled in northern France since 911.

The Domesday Book
People began calling it this because, like the Day of Judgment, there could be no appeal against its contents. ('Doom' meant 'judgment'.)

WILLIAM II (Rufus)
1087-1100 (b. 1056)
HENRY I (Beauclerc)
1100-1135 (b. 1068)

A motte and bailey castle

This was the earliest type of Norman castle. The 'motte' was the mound on which the wooden keep, the strong central part of the castle, was built.

The 'bailey' was a fenced area where the household lived, and storerooms and workshops were located. By 1100 William had fortified England with over 5,000 castles.

William II and Henry I

William Rufus was a brave and practical king who spent much of his reign trying to win Normandy from his older brother, Robert. Henry, the third and youngest brother, sided with both in turn. In 1091 William and Robert made peace; but their **treaty** collapsed after William broke his promise to help Robert in battle. In 1096 Robert 'lent' Normandy to William in return for 10,000 marks (a very large sum of money in those days) while Robert went on a **Crusade**.

Whether William would have given Normandy back is unknown, for in 1100 he died. His younger brother, Henry, was crowned within days. Henry promised to maintain peace and justice, and he worked hard at running England more efficiently. He loved the Church and encouraged learning; at that time the two were connected, because most books were written and copied out by monks.

Because of this, Henry was nicknamed 'Beauclerc' ('good scholar' in French). In 1101, Henry gave most of Normandy back to Robert, to stop him from trying to take the English throne. The brothers remained enemies, however, and in 1106 Henry defeated Robert at the battle of Tinchebrai, Normandy. Robert was Henry's prisoner for the rest of his life, and Henry ruled Normandy.

Henry was the only one of the three brothers to marry. He had twins, William and Matilda; he also had a favourite nephew, Stephen of Blois. In 1120 his son William was drowned in a shipwreck, and Matilda became the heir to the English throne. When her husband, the **Holy Roman Emperor**, died, Henry married her to Geoffrey Plantagenet, Count of Anjou, by whom she had three sons.

In 1135 Geoffrey angered Henry by asking for part of Normandy, but Henry died before their quarrel was resolved.

The sinking of the 'White Ship'
Henry's son, William, was on this ship when it was wrecked in 1120. William was drowned.

Fountains Abbey, North Yorkshire, England
Henry built magnificent abbeys: some are now in ruins but still beautiful.

STEPHEN
1135-1154
(b. 1097)

Matilda

By her second marriage she was Countess of Anjou. But her first husband, who had died, had been the Holy Roman Emperor, and she preferred to call herself 'Empress Matilda'. Her son Henry by her second marriage (later Henry II) was known as 'Henry Fitzempress' (Henry, son of the empress), rather than 'Henry of Anjou'.

Stephen

Before he died, Henry I had said that his daughter Matilda should succeed him. This was unusual as women did not normally rule in England. There were many people who were against Matilda becoming queen.

When Henry died, the throne was offered to Matilda's cousin, Stephen of Blois. He was liked by the people for his courage and good nature.

On 22 December 1135, Stephen was crowned king. He was not a wise king, and in 1138 civil war began as Earl Robert of Gloucester, Henry I's eldest **illegitimate** son, led a rebellion aimed at making Matilda queen. She came to England from France in 1139, and in 1141 Stephen was imprisoned.

Matilda was chosen as queen, but her greedy actions angered the people so much that she was not crowned, and was instead driven out of London. Civil war raged for eight more years. Then in 1147, Earl Robert of Gloucester died, and Matilda fled.

Stephen remained a weak king. Matilda's husband, Geoffrey Plantagenet, did well, becoming Duke of Normandy in 1144. In 1153 their son, Henry, invaded England. Stephen's own son, Eustace, died, and Stephen made peace with Henry Plantagenet by declaring him heir to the throne.

Stephen and the little hostage

In 1152 the leader of a castle Stephen was attacking asked for a truce. Stephen was given a five-year-old boy as a **hostage**. *The truce was broken but Stephen spared the boy, although he had been urged to catapult him back into the castle. The boy later recalled playing 'knights' – a game like conkers – with King Stephen, using plantain stalks he had picked from the grass.*

THE NORMANS

HENRY II
1154-1189 (b. 1133)

Thomas Becket's murder

Becket was Henry's friend. But after Henry made him Archbishop of Canterbury, he resisted Henry's attempts to reduce the Church's power. In 1170, Henry, in a rage, begged for someone to get rid of Becket. At once four knights rode away; Henry sent a man to stop them, but it was too late, and they murdered Becket in his cathedral. Becket was later made a saint.

Henry II

Henry II was the great-grandson of William the Conqueror. He also ruled the French regions of Normandy, Aquitaine, Anjou, and Maine. He was the first of the Plantagenet kings. The name 'Plantagenet' is from the Latin planta genesta, which means 'broom'. Henry's father (Geoffrey of Anjou) loved hunting so much that he planted broom all over his land to encourage game to breed and live in its cover. It is also said that he wore a sprig of broom in his helmet.

Henry II was highly intelligent, active, efficient, and hot-tempered. Aquitaine and Maine were Henry's through his marriage to Eleanor of Aquitaine. She was famed for her beauty, and her intelligence and spirit matched Henry's.

Henry's aim was to restore England to what it had been under Henry I. He retook lost territories, and destroyed castles built without permission. He improved the economy and legal system, creating the *Curia Regis*, or King's Court, which travelled around the country so that **freemen** could seek justice there. He also founded a system of six travelling **assizes**. He introduced trial by jury, and began the use of Westminster as a centre of government.

Henry was not such a good father, and his discontented sons plotted against him. His marriage to Eleanor turned sour, and she joined her favourite son, Richard, in plotting against Henry. In 1173, after Eleanor had aided three of their sons in a rebellion, Henry placed her in honourable confinement. There she remained until Henry's death.

In 1183 Henry's heir, 'Young King' Henry, died. Richard was now the eldest and the natural heir. But Henry would not proclaim him heir, nor let him go on Crusade. Richard angrily enlisted the help of King Philip II of France, and attacked his father's French territories. When Henry, ill and exhausted from fighting, learnt that his favourite son, John, had joined Richard, he died, broken-hearted.

Oxford University
In 1167 Oxford became important as a centre of learning, when the University of Paris banned English students.

Henry's queen, Eleanor of Aquitaine
Eleanor was famed for her beauty, brilliant mind, and courage.

**RICHARD I
(Coeur-de-lion)**
1189-1199 (b. 1157)

Eleanor, Richard's mother, and Richard's ransom
This pile of treasure was the 150,000 marks (35 tons) the English raised to buy Richard out of captivity in Austria.

A fictional picture of Richard fighting Saladin
In reality they never met.

Richard I

Richard was handsome, brave, tall and strong. Because of his bravery in battle, he became known as 'Coeur-de-lion', meaning 'Lion-heart'.

His first action as king was to free his mother Eleanor, and send her to England to rule until he arrived from France. Richard was crowned in September 1189, and left England that December as co-leader of the Third Crusade. Richard was hero-worshipped for his fighting ability, and because Crusaders were thought of as heroic, noble, and close to God. In fact, Richard behaved with great savagery whilst fighting the Muslims. In 1191 Richard and his army besieged the city of Acre, in Palestine. Richard was keen to move on to Jerusalem, and lost patience while waiting for a ransom to be paid.

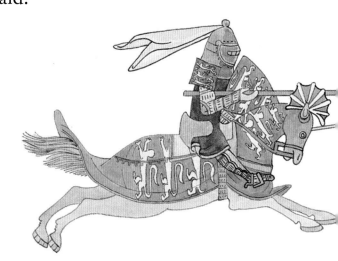

So he chained up all 3,000 citizens of Acre, including women and children, and ordered them to be slaughtered. Saladin, the leader of the Muslims, was a man of honour and had never committed so cruel an act.

After the Third Crusade, Richard hurried to France to defend his territories there. He loved, but did not trust, his brother John. Richard gave John land in Normandy, and **revenues** in England, to satisfy John's thirst for power and wealth. Even so, John tried to overthrow Richard's government, but received no support from the barons, who admired Richard. John then supported Richard against King Philip II of France.

Richard spoke only French, and spent no more than six months of the ten years of his reign in England. He died in France of gangrene from an arrow wound in the shoulder.

These unlucky omens shadowed Richard's reign:
1 His father's corpse bled at the nose when he neared it. It was said that a corpse bled only in the presence of its murderer.
2 A bat flew around him in daylight at his coronation.
3 His sacred Crusader's staff broke when he leaned upon it.

JOHN (Lackland)
1199-1216 (b. 1167)

Part of a painting of King John hunting

John loved hunting. He took away the rights of his subjects to hunt or grow food in the royal forests, so that he could hunt in peace. This increased the barons' anger.

John

John was unpopular because of his history of plotting against family members and betraying allies. He was not glamorous, or religious, or a great warrior. He inherited a kingdom made penniless by Richard I's expensive foreign wars.

John did not do much to improve matters, but he did run the government very efficiently. He cared about just laws, especially for poor people.

In 1208 John rejected the Pope's choice, Stephen Langton, as Archbishop of Canterbury. In anger, the Pope banned all religious rites in England, except for baptism and **last rites**. In response, John seized church property and wealth. In 1209, as punishment for this, the Pope **excommunicated** John, and in 1213 told King Philip II of France to invade England. At this, John gave in and finally swore obedience to the Pope, who lifted his ban. Stephen Langton's first act as Archbishop was to lift John's excommunication.

John was unlucky in war. He lost most of England's land in France, and so he lived up to his nickname, 'Lackland'.

In 1215 John signed a treaty with the barons. It was later called the 'Magna Carta' (which is Latin for 'Great Charter'). It is famous for including a promise that all people should have the right to justice. Never before had a king of England signed such a treaty.

The powerful barons hated John's heavy taxes, especially **scutage**, and in 1214 they rose against him. In 1215, in Runnymede meadow by the River Thames, John signed a treaty with the barons. A few months later, John persuaded the Pope to release him from the promises made in the treaty. The barons were still very angry and fought John. In 1216, exhausted with fighting, John died of a fever.

A jewelled cup
Part of John's treasures lost in 1216 when some baggage wagons fell into the Nene estuary. It was recently recovered.

HENRY III
1216-1272 (b. 1207)

William Marshal's tomb in the Temple Church, London

Marshal was famed throughout the Christian world for his courage, physical power and skill in fighting, and also for his honourable nature. He served Henry II, Richard I and John with utter loyalty. Peers and churchmen alike respected his wisdom and asked his advice. Finally, in his 70s, he ruled as Regent for the boy-king, Henry III.

Henry III

Henry was only nine years old when he became king. So William Marshal, Earl of Pembroke, acted as **Regent** until his death in 1219, when another Regent took over until 1227. They ruled the country for the young Henry. Marshal was a giant in strength, sense, and loyalty. He had been the little hostage whose life King Stephen had spared (see page 25). Strong in battle, and a loving and unselfish servant, he served Henry II, Richard I, and John with great loyalty.

Unfortunately, Henry was a weak king: foolish and dishonourable. Unlucky in war, he failed to regain England's territories in France lost by King John.

Henry's wife, Eleanor, was French. She brought French nobles to the English court. Henry showed special favour to these Frenchmen, often giving them English land. This made them hated by the English barons. The high taxes Henry demanded, and his wasting money on useless wars, made things even worse.

In 1258 Simon de Montfort, Henry's brother-in-law, led the barons in demanding changes to the government.

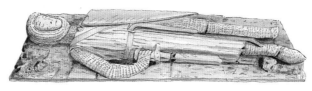

De Montfort insisted that Henry banish his French favourites. Henry promised to meet these demands, called 'the Provisions of Oxford'.

In 1261 the Pope gave Henry permission to break his promise, and in 1264 civil war broke out. Henry was captured and Simon de Montfort ruled, until he was killed in 1265 in battle with Prince Edward, Henry's son.

Prince Edward was now more powerful in reality than his father, and his promises of fair government, through a parliament, had brought him supporters in the fight against de Montfort. In practice, Edward now became ruler of the country.

Henry spent his last years enjoying his happy and long marriage, and encouraging the arts. He was a lover of architecture and many beautiful cathedrals were built or improved during his reign. Westminster Abbey was rebuilt and Edward the Confessor's remains were reburied there.

Simon de Montfort's government
He introduced the 'Council of Nine'. These nine people advised the king. Ordinary citizens took part in government for the first time.

Henry overseeing the rebuilding of Westminster Abbey
The Abbey has been central to the history of England. Every English monarch since William I has been crowned there.

EDWARD I
(Longshanks)
1272-1307 (b. 1239)

Edward I

Edward I was a fine warrior, and won the respect of his subjects. He was very tall and strong, and his nickname, 'Longshanks', referred to his long legs.

He had helped his father, Henry III, to govern since he was twelve, and he had also been a Crusader. He stamped out corruption in government, and in 1295 established a 'Model Parliament'– the first to include clergy, nobles, and commoners. He also changed the legal system.

In 1282 Edward defeated and killed the Welsh prince, Llywelyn, the last of the Welsh royal line. As a recompense, it is said, Edward offered his baby son (also called Edward) to the Welsh people as their prince, at Caernarfon Castle in 1284.

Conwy Castle
The conquest of Wales took five years. Edward made sure of his victory by building fortress castles there, such as this one.

Edward showing his baby son to the Welsh people
This may not really have happened, but it is said that Edward promised the Welsh 'a prince who speaks no English'; the baby Edward could not yet speak at all. In 1301 the young prince was officially created Prince of Wales.

In 13th-century Europe, hatred of Jewish people reached a peak. (The Jews were blamed for Jesus' death, although Jesus was Jewish.) Jews were banned from most jobs and so often became money lenders. English kings relied on them for funds. But Edward I found money elsewhere, and in 1290 he expelled the 3,000 English Jews and took their land.

Edward was determined to conquer Scotland as well as Wales. He gained the title 'Hammer of the Scots', fighting the Scots from 1296 until his death.

Persecution of Jews, from a 13th-century picture
Jews had to wear yellow badges to mark them out.

EDWARD II
1307-1327 (b. 1284)

Robert Bruce, the Scottish king at the Battle of Bannockburn, 1314

Bruce's victory there assured Scottish independence. Throughout the rest of Edward's reign, Bruce and his armies attacked northern England.

Edward II

The unfortunate Edward II was neither wise nor popular. He had no military success in Scotland or France, and his favouritism towards the handsome Frenchman, Piers Gaveston, infuriated the nobles. Edward even left the rude Gaveston in charge in his place in 1308 while he went to marry Isabella, Princess of France. The barons were so insulted and angry at having Gaveston set above them that they forced Edward to banish him to Ireland. But in 1312 Edward brought him back. There was a revolt in which Gaveston was captured and murdered. By 1321 Edward had new favourites, Hugh Despenser and his power-hungry son, also called Hugh.

This caused civil war and Parliament banished the Despensers. Edward won a battle in 1322, and foolishly executed the opposition leader, the Earl of Lancaster (this was the first time that a **peer** had been executed).

In 1325 Queen Isabella went to France, and returned with her lover, Roger Mortimer, and an army. They killed the Despensers, imprisoned Edward, and proclaimed the king's young son 'Keeper of the Realm'. Edward II **abdicated** and his son (also called Edward) became king. Mortimer, it is said, saw to it that Edward II was horribly murdered, with a red-hot poker.

Edward and Piers Gaveston
Edward was not interested in governing; he preferred sports or gardening with his favourite, Gaveston. He even gave Gaveston some of his wedding presents, which hurt his wife's feelings.

Hungry people forced to leave their homes as crop failures in 1314 and 1315 brought famine
Food shortages and high prices lasted until 1318.

Edward claimed the throne of France and added the French fleur-de-lys symbol on his coat of arms.

The Black Death (bubonic plague)

This swept England and the rest of Europe from 1348 to 1350. One in three people died. The plague was spread by fleas from black rats. This is a 14th-century picture of plague victims being buried.

Edward III

Edward III took over the government of England from Isabella, his mother, and Roger Mortimer in 1330. His first concern was to avenge his father's shameful death. He executed Mortimer, and compelled Isabella to spend the rest of her days at Castle Rising, in Norfolk.

Edward's reign was a long and great one. He reformed the law, improving justice for ordinary people. He made English, not French, the official language of law and Parliament. He was also successful in war, regaining almost a quarter of France with the help of his warrior son Edward, the Black Prince (so called because he wore black armour).

King Edward's determination to claim the French throne from his uncle, the childless French king Charles IV, brought about the beginning of the **Hundred Years War** (1337-1453).

One of the main reasons for Edward's military success was the use of the longbow. Only English archers had it. In 1346 the brilliance of the longbowmen brought England victory at the battle of Crécy, France. Because of this, Calais surrendered to Edward in 1347.

By 1374 only Calais and a tiny strip of southwestern France remained in English hands. Edward did also make a few gains in Scotland. He captured the Scots king, David. David was ransomed by his people, and kept the peace with Edward. The Black Prince died in 1376, and his heartbroken father died the following year.

Edward daydreaming of Arthur's knights
He wanted to create a court like that of the legendary King Arthur, with a Round Table where all were equal and courage, honour, and kindness to the weak were valued above all else.

The badge of the knightly 'Order of the Garter'
When a court lady's garter fell off as she danced, Edward stopped people's laughter by picking it up, putting it on his leg, and saying 'Honi soit qui mal y pense' ('Shame on him who thinks badly of it'). He created the Order, with those words as its motto.

THE PLANTAGENETS

RICHARD II
1377-1399 (b. 1367)

Geoffrey Chaucer, author of 'The Canterbury Tales'

He was one of Richard's friends. In his great book, pilgrims travelling to Canterbury each tell a comical tale.

Richard II

Richard, son of Edward the Black Prince, was another weak king, though he was brave and showed skill in dealing with other rulers. He brought peace to Ireland, and made a truce with France. He was also a lover of the arts. His big failings were a hasty temper and the belief a king could do as he liked.

Richard was only ten when he became king, and his uncle, John of Gaunt, governed as Regent until 1389. In 1397 Richard made himself 'absolute monarch', taking power away from Parliament. In 1399 he went too far when he banished his cousin Henry Bolingbroke, (John of Gaunt's son) and took Henry's inheritance after John of Gaunt's death.

Henry returned from France with an army, imprisoned Richard, and forced him to abdicate. Richard was an only child, and had no children. The next in line to the throne, Edmund Mortimer, was only eight. Parliament declared Henry as the next king.

In 1400, a revolt by Richard's supporters was put down. Following this, Richard was imprisoned in Pontefract Castle and murdered there. He was the last Plantagenet king.

The pilgrims on their way to Canterbury

Richard calms the furious peasants

A high **poll tax**, introduced in 1380, led to the Peasants' Revolt of 1381. The revolt, led by a man named Wat Tyler, ended when Richard spoke to the angry crowd who poured through London, looting and burning.

When the Lord Mayor killed Wat Tyler in trying to arrest him, the 14-year-old Richard showed enormous courage. He rode into the angry crowd alone, leading the people away with him, and so prevented a **massacre**.

THE PLANTAGENETS

HENRY IV (Bolingbroke)
1399-1413 (b. 1367)

Sheep farmers at work shearing

A fall in wool prices created problems for Henry. The tax on these exports had been one of the main sources of royal income.

Henry IV

Henry IV was a well-educated, good-mannered man who loved reading. But his reign was bloody and difficult. The first crisis of his reign was a revolt led by the murdered Richard II's half-brother.

As king, Henry had to deal with rebellions in Wales and Scotland. Owain Glyndwr, the Welsh leader, revolted. So did the Earl of Northumberland, and his son Harry Percy (known as 'Hotspur' because of his temper and love of war). In 1403 Hotspur and his father led an uprising against Henry, who owed them money. Owain Glyndwr and Hotspur were related by marriage, and planned to join forces. Henry was determined to prevent this. Hotspur was killed at the Battle of Shrewsbury.

Henry could hardly afford all this costly fighting.

To make it worse, Henry's enemies helped one another, and in 1405 the King of France invaded, along with Glyndwr. Henry resisted them all, but soon he became ill. From then on, his son Henry, a fine soldier, took more responsibility, defeating and executing the Earl of Northumberland in 1408, and governing from 1409.

Henry's illness scarred his skin and paralysed him. Many believed it was God's punishment for the murder of Richard II. Henry felt guilty about Richard's death, and spent many hours praying in Westminster Abbey.

Owain Glyndwr, the Welsh leader

Glyndwr was a thorn in Henry's side. He was proclaimed Prince of Wales in 1400, and led a revolt that year. He supported the Earl of Northumberland's uprising in 1403, and helped the French to invade in 1405. In 1408 Henry, Prince of Wales, killed Glyndwr's ally, Northumberland. In 1410 Glyndwr abandoned his rebellion.

THE LANCASTRIANS

HENRY V
1413-1422 (b. 1387)

The English longbow
It was much faster than the French crossbow.

Agincourt, 1415
This battle has made Henry immortal. He so inspired his men, an army mostly of archers, that they shattered the resistance of a huge French force.

Henry V

Henry V was loved and honoured by his people. Like his father (Henry IV), he loved the arts. He showed great self-discipline, was astoundingly successful in war, and very religious. He was generous to his father's opponents, and reburied the murdered Richard II with honour.

Henry's personality changed when he became king; he had led a wild, fun-loving life as Prince of Wales. As king, he behaved in a sensible, thoughtful, dignified, and mature manner. Henry's reign began with plots against him, but the conspirators were caught and executed. He continued the Hundred Years War against France, begun by Edward III. In 1415, Henry and his army sailed to France. They captured the town of Harfleur in September. By October they were exhausted.

Many were ill and they had very little food left.

Henry was a brilliant leader. He arranged his army so intelligently, and inspired them so powerfully that at the battle of Agincourt, near Calais, they defeated a mounted French army three to five times the size of the English force. More brilliant victories followed, until in 1419 the French king made peace. Later, the two kings signed a treaty, which allowed Henry to keep all the land he had conquered. It also gave him the French king's daughter, Catherine, in marriage, and said Henry should become the next King of France.

= English possessions in France in 1422.

The victorious Henry
Here he forces King Charles VI of France to make him heir to the French throne in 1420. Henry died before he could be crowned King of France.

HENRY VI
1422-1461
1470-1471 (b. 1421)

The Wars of the Roses

These were fought from 1455 to 1485, between the Lancastrians (whose badge was a red rose) and the Yorkists (whose badge was a white rose).

THE LANCASTRIANS

Henry VI

Henry VI, son of Henry V, was only a baby when he came to the throne. His great-uncle acted as Regent until Henry was crowned king when he was nine years old.

Henry was better fitted to be a monk than a king. His reign was a chapter of disasters. England lost almost all her French territories again. This caused such anger that in 1450 the common people rebelled, led by a man named Jack Cade.

Margaret of Anjou

Disastrously for Henry, in 1455 the battle for the throne began between the Houses of Lancaster and York. Henry was the great-grandson of Edward III's son, John of Gaunt. John's son had been Duke of Lancaster. But Edmund Mortimer was descended through a female line, from an older son of Edward III and he thought he should be king. Many supported him. Mortimer's nephew, Edward, Duke of York, fought against Henry. This struggle, later called the **Wars of the Roses**, continued, on and off, for the next thirty years.

Henry's queen, Margaret of Anjou, was a good leader. She led Henry's forces against the Yorkists with courage and vigour. But Henry was captured twice, and in 1461 he was deposed, in favour of Edward, Duke of York, who had himself crowned Edward IV.

After being deposed, Henry wandered the country in exile, until in 1470 Margaret returned with an army and captured King Edward. Henry VI became king for the second time, but the people were against him. In 1471 he was again deposed after a defeat at the Battle of Tewkesbury, where his son was killed. The king was imprisoned in the Tower of London, and murdered there.

Joan of Arc
This peasant girl who had visions of freedom for France led the French armies to victory over Henry's men at Orléans in 1429. In 1431 French churchmen who supported the English burnt her at the stake as a witch.

Henry sings and dances under a tree during a battle
In 1453 Henry had a period of madness. He wore humble clothes, disliking the grandeur of royal show.

THE LANCASTRIANS

A printing press
William Caxton set up the first press in 1476. Printing completely changed society.

The House of York

Edward IV was another tall, handsome, warrior king. The scheming Earl of Warwick had helped Edward to the throne by deposing Henry VI in 1461. Warwick did not like Edward's wife, Elizabeth Woodville, who was a commoner. Nor did he like the power Edward gave to her family, so in 1470 he betrayed Edward and helped Queen Margaret to restore her husband, Henry VI, to the throne. Edward defeated them at the Battle of Tewkesbury. Henry VI was murdered soon afterwards.

Edward IV returned to the throne, and the rest of his reign was peaceful and prosperous, for him and for England.

Edward V had almost no reign. His so-called 'Protector', his uncle Richard of Gloucester, declared Edward's parents' marriage invalid, and that therefore the 12-year-old Edward should not be king. Richard was made king instead. Edward and his younger brother were held inside the Tower of London. The two children were seen playing there until July 1483, when they disappeared.

Richard III's reign was short, and shadowed by the terrible suspicion that he had had his little nephews murdered.

It seemed only a matter of time before Henry Tudor, of the Lancastrian line, would claim the throne. In 1485 Henry Tudor invaded, and met Richard III at the Battle of Bosworth Field. Many of Richard's men deserted, and he was defeated and killed. He had begun his reign betraying his brother and the two nephews entrusted to his care. He ended it fighting bravely, but in shame. His dead body was taken away naked and dirty, slung over a horse's back.

Edward V at confession

*His doctor said that Edward confessed and did **penance** daily, expecting to be killed soon.*

Elizabeth Woodville

She was not of royal blood, but her beauty captured Edward IV's heart. This marriage, of king and commoner, provided the scheming Richard III with an excuse to depose her son, Edward V.

Richard III's body being led away on horseback after the Battle of Bosworth Field, in 1485.

THE YORKS

The Ladybird Book of

KINGS & QUEENS
OF ENGLAND

Part 2
1485 – The Present Day

HENRY VII
1485-1509 (b. 1457)

The impostor Lambert Simnel
He had to work as a kitchen boy in Henry's kitchens.

Henry created this court of justice
It was named the Court of the Star Chamber after the stars painted on its ceiling.

Henry VII

Henry Tudor's victory over Richard III at the Battle of Bosworth Field, in 1485, ended thirty years of bitter fighting for the crown between the House of Lancaster and the House of York. This struggle is known as the Wars of the Roses.

Henry VII was a Lancastrian. To make sure peace continued, in the year after the Battle of Bosworth Field, he married Elizabeth of York. She was the eldest daughter of the late Edward IV, a Yorkist king. Henry's marriage to Elizabeth united the feuding houses of Lancaster and York, and in this way he became the first king of a new royal house. This new house became known as 'Tudor', from Henry's surname.

The early years of Henry's reign were still troubled by Yorkist claims to the throne.

Two claimants were impostors: the first, Lambert Simnel, had been coached by a group of Yorkists to pretend that he was Edward IV's nephew. The 12-year old Simnel was crowned Edward VI in Dublin in 1487. But in the same year Henry defeated the plotters and made Simnel a kitchen-hand. The other impostor, Perkin Warbeck, troubled Henry for much longer. Warbeck was arrested in 1497, but continued his trouble-making even in captivity. He was executed in 1499.

Henry was a strong, learned and thoughtful king, who was fair in law giving and very good at making and keeping money. His long reign brought peace and prosperity but he was never much loved by his subjects, as he lacked warmth and charm.

Pembroke Castle (Wales)

Henry's birthplace, and his personal standard, the red dragon of Wales. Henry was Welsh on his father's side.

Perkin Warbeck's execution

Warbeck enlisted the support of many foreign rulers for his claim to be Richard, brother of the tragic Edward V (the boy-king who had been imprisoned and died in the Tower of London).

THE TUDORS

HENRY VIII
1509-1547 (b. 1491)

With the voyages of the great explorers, the wealth of distant lands could be acquired. In 1524, turkeys were brought from South America.

One of the warships Henry had built in 1511, when he overhauled the Royal Navy
Each ship weighed 1,000 tons.

Henry VIII

Henry VII had two sons. Arthur, the elder son, had died young, and so his brother Henry became the next king.

Henry VIII was handsome and charming, and was welcomed by the people. He married Arthur's young widow, the Spanish Catherine of Aragon, and seemed destined for a happy reign. But after twenty years he became obsessed with the need for a son and **heir**, and wanted a new wife. The Church did not allow divorce. Henry claimed that his marriage was not valid, because marriage to a brother's widow was not allowed (he had had special permission for his marriage).

Catherine of Aragon

Anne Boleyn

Jane Seymour

Anne of Cleves

Catherine Howard

Catherine Parr

The Pope would not agree to a divorce, and so Henry officially denied the Pope's authority and divorced Catherine.

In 1531 Henry broke away from the Roman Catholic Church and declared himself head of a separate English Church. He closed the monasteries in England and took their treasures. Yet he was not sympathetic to Protestants, believing himself a Catholic despite his actions.

Henry married five more times after his divorce from Catherine. Of his six wives only Jane Seymour bore him the son he wanted. She died in childbirth.

Henry was a wilful, powerful man, who changed the course of English history to get what he wanted, and killed those who displeased him.

Henry's pursuit of a son and heir

To ensure the continuation of the new Tudor line Henry married six times. He seemed happy with Edward VI's mother, Jane Seymour, but she died giving birth to Edward. He divorced Anne of Cleves for being too ugly; Catherine Howard lost her head for being unfaithful to him. Edward remained his only son.

THE TUDORS

EDWARD VI
1547-1553 (b. 1537)

Edward VI

Edward was only ten when his father died, so government was in the hands of a group of lords called the Regency Council. Edward's uncle, the Duke of Somerset, bribed other Council members to put him in charge, with the title Lord Protector. Somerset was very ambitious, but also kind and indecisive.

16th-century village life had been disrupted by 'enclosure'. This was the hedging and fencing of land so that the landowners could keep sheep on it. The peasants were angry and worried. In 1549, many rebelled. Robert Kett, a Norfolk man, led 16,000 rebels. Somerset's delay in setting the army on the rebels lost him support from the **aristocracy**, and the ruthless Duke of Northumberland took his place.

Land enclosure riots

Public anger grew throughout the 16th century, as landowners fenced off land that had been in common use. In 1549, rioting erupted countrywide.

Northumberland was ambitious and selfish. The English Protestant Church was established in 1549-52, and Northumberland punished and imprisoned many loyal Catholics. He also married one of his sons to Lady Jane Grey, a sweet-natured and brilliant granddaughter of Henry VIII's younger sister. Edward fell gravely ill with tuberculosis. Northumberland persuaded him to make Lady Jane his heir, claiming that Henry VIII's marriages to Catherine of Aragon, Mary's mother, and Anne Boleyn, Elizabeth's mother, had been **invalid**. Edward died and on 10 July 1553 the unwilling Lady Jane was named queen. Supporters rallied to Edward's half-sister, Princess Mary, and on 19 July 1553 the Regency Council declared her queen instead. Lady Jane, her husband, and Northumberland were imprisoned, found guilty of **treason**, and condemned to death.

Edward founded Christ's Hospital School, known as the Bluecoat School.

Lady Jane Grey
Her father and the Duke of Northumberland plotted to make her queen. The 15-year-old Jane fainted when told she was queen, four days after Edward's death.

Thomas Cranmer, the first Protestant Archbishop of Canterbury

He was burned at the stake in 1556.

Mary I

Mary's first acts as queen were to have the scheming Northumberland executed, and then to re-establish the Catholic Church; for Mary was a Catholic like her mother, Catherine of Aragon.

At first, Mary behaved fairly towards convinced Protestants. But in 1554 Sir Thomas Wyatt led a rebellion in protest against Mary's planned marriage to Philip, Catholic heir to the throne of Spain. Lady Jane Grey's father was among the rebels. Mary executed over 100 people, including the innocent Lady Jane and her husband. She even suspected her own sister Elizabeth and imprisoned her.

Mary then married Philip. After a year Philip left to rule Spain. The unhappy Mary tried to convert the whole kingdom to Catholicism. She **persecuted** Protestants, and burned many at the stake. This earned her the nickname 'Bloody Mary'.

In 1557 Mary and Philip went to war against France, and in 1558 the French won Calais, the last of England's French territories. Mary died brokenhearted, for English rule in France was dear to her.

Road works in Mary's reign
She reformed the country's financial affairs and improved its roads.

English whaling boat
In 1557 English whale fishing started at Spitzbergen, Norway.

THE TUDORS

ELIZABETH I
1558-1603 (b. 1533)

The execution of Mary, Queen of Scots

Mary had been Elizabeth's captive for nineteen years. Elizabeth did not want her executed, although Mary had plotted against her, but she had to give the order. Elizabeth was furious that her order to kill Mary had been carried out, however, and punished the official who had sent the order through.

Elizabeth I

Elizabeth I was a wise and careful **monarch**. She chose excellent advisers, Sir William Cecil, better known as Lord Burghley and later his son Robert Cecil. She restored the Protestant religion, and made herself supreme head of a single English church, as her father Henry VIII had done. Her Catholic cousin Mary, the Scottish queen, became a threat to her. When Mary's husband Francis became king of France, Mary called herself 'Queen of England and Scotland'. King Francis died in 1560 and Mary returned to Scotland. She was soon **deposed** and imprisoned on suspicion of helping in the murder of her second husband, Lord Darnley.

Mary escaped, and asked for Elizabeth's help. Elizabeth kept her semi-captive. But Mary remained the focus of Catholic plotting. In 1586 Mary was found to have joined in a plot, led by Anthony Babington, to kill Elizabeth. Reluctantly, Elizabeth had Mary executed. Mary met her death with great courage, even when the first blow of the axe failed to go through her neck, and she whispered, 'Sweet Jesus'.

Elizabeth never married, although early in her reign it seemed that she might wed her favourite, Robert Dudley, after the sudden and mysterious death of his wife. Dudley stayed her favourite until his death in 1588.

William Shakespeare (1564–1616), England's greatest dramatist
His plays were performed in the Globe Theatre, London.

In the 1560s, English merchant seamen began to capture African people and sell them as slaves.

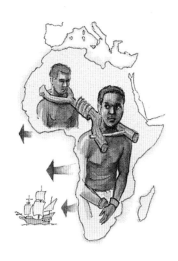

THE TUDORS

ELIZABETH I
1558-1603 (b. 1533)

During Elizabeth's reign exploration flourished, and new places and people were discovered. Sir Walter Raleigh brought tobacco and potatoes to England from America.

In 1579, Elizabeth came close to marrying the French Duke of Alençon. The English disliked the idea of foreign interference, and still fiercely opposed the Catholic religion (which Alençon followed); so Elizabeth gave up the idea of marriage although she had other favourites, including Sir Walter Raleigh and the Earl of Essex. She became known as 'The Virgin Queen', and Sir Walter Raleigh named the American state of Virginia after her when he claimed it for England.

Elizabeth's reign saw a flowering of the arts, invention, and exploration. Her court welcomed English musicians, painters and poets. The period also saw the emergence of some of the greatest English writers, such as William Shakespeare and Christopher Marlowe. The first flush lavatory was also invented. In 1581 the explorer Francis Drake was knighted, after completing the first English round-the-world voyage.

Later Sir Walter Raleigh set off in search of **El Dorado**.

In 1588, angered by Elizabeth's treatment of Catholics, by Mary Queen of Scots' execution, and by English interference in a war between Spain and Holland, King Philip of Spain sent a war fleet, the Armada, to attack England. The weather was against the Spanish, and the English, commanded by Sir Francis Drake, easily defeated them off the coast of France; a second Armada, six years later, was scattered by storms.

Elizabeth gradually paid all of England's debts, and was able to reduce taxes in the 1570s. War was expensive, though, and the Spanish war sent the treasury back into debt. It remained in debt at Elizabeth's death, though the amount was not great.

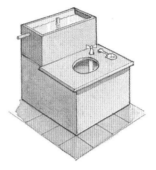

The first flush lavatory

It was built about 1595 near Bath by Sir John Harrington, Elizabeth's godson. Elizabeth is said to have ordered one. It had a sloping bowl made of lead or stone and a wooden seat, and a clamp to stop people flushing it just for fun.

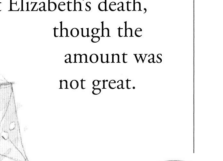

Sir Francis Drake and the Spanish Armada

JAMES I
1603-1625 (b. 1566)

The 'Authorised Version' of the Bible
In 1611 James authorised a translation of the Bible from Latin into English. This translation is still in use today.

Guy Fawkes is caught preparing to blow up the Houses of Parliament in 1605.

James I

James, son of Mary, Queen of Scots, was already king of Scotland and he was a witty and wise speaker. The English people were tired of Elizabeth, who could be fussy and a ditherer, and welcomed him gladly. James behaved harshly to Catholics and to a group of extreme Protestants, the **Puritans**, and several Catholic plots against him were exposed. The most famous was the Gunpowder Plot, discovered in 1605 when Guy Fawkes and other Catholics were found in the cellars of the **House of Commons** preparing to blow up King James and Parliament.

These plots increased public sympathy for James, but not for long. His deeds were not as wise as his words. He believed in the **Divine Right of Kings**, and so thought he had God's authority.

He argued with Parliament over everything. In 1614 Parliament was called 'The Addled Parliament' because they could not agree on anything, and so no Acts could be passed. After this James ruled without Parliament.

He continued to persecute Puritans, and in 1620 a group of them, later known as the 'Pilgrim Fathers', sailed to America in the Mayflower to escape him. They founded a settlement in Pennsylvania.

Then in 1621 James had to recall Parliament because he needed money to help his son-in-law, the Dutch king, to repel a Spanish invasion.

James became very unpopular. He seemed weak and foolish, and was devoted to his favourite, the Duke of Buckingham. He was also very fond of drinking.

Sir Walter Raleigh James imprisoned him for treason. In 1616 he released him to look for El Dorado. (James needed money.) In 1618 Raleigh returned empty-handed and James had him executed.

THE STUARTS

The first use of wallpaper, as a cheap alternative to tapestry, was in about 1645.

Charles I

Charles inherited a mess from his father, and he repeated many of James's mistakes. Like his father, he believed that he ruled by God's command. In 1629 he too dissolved Parliament, and ruled without it until 1640. He raised money by forcing loans from the wealthy, selling knighthoods, and with many unfair and unpopular taxes. He took more notice of his father's favourite, the Duke of Buckingham, than of wise advisers. Buckingham's pride and temper led Charles into costly wars with France and Spain. But in 1628 Buckingham was murdered, and Charles began to follow the advice of his queen, Henrietta Maria. This did not please Protestants, for the queen was a Catholic. In 1638 a group of Scottish Protestants made a solemn vow (called the '**Covenant**') to defend their religion against Charles's attempts to change it, and in 1640 they invaded England. Charles fell out with his new Parliament, and dismissed it.

In 1642, Charles took soldiers to the House of Commons to arrest five members of the House for plotting with the Covenanters. But they had been warned and had fled. Charles realised that Parliament was against him, and left London. He gathered his supporters, known as the Royalists, and declared war on Parliament. During this Civil War, Oliver Cromwell emerged as a fine general and in 1644 trained the '**New Model Army**'. It defeated the Royalist forces, and in 1646 Charles surrendered in Scotland and was handed over to his enemies. In January 1649 Charles was tried and executed.

Bananas were on sale in shops in Britain for the first time in 1633.

Charles's execution
He wore two shirts, so that he would not shiver with cold and seem frightened. He also asked the executioner not to cut off his beard, as it had 'caused no offence'. His calm dignity moved and impressed everyone who saw or heard of it.

THE STUARTS

CHARLES II
1660-1685 (b. 1630)

Many English pubs are called the 'Royal Oak'

They are named after the great oak tree in which Charles II hid after his defeat at the Battle of Worcester.

Charles II

Charles's heir, also named Charles, took the oath of the Covenant in 1650 in Scotland, and was proclaimed king by the Scots. He gathered supporters and in 1651 joined battle against the **Parliamentarians**. He was defeated at the Battle of Worcester, and fled to join his mother in France.

In 1653 Oliver Cromwell made himself head of state, and became as tyrannical as any king. He was a strict Puritan and banned entertainment and the wearing of bright colours. In 1655 he dissolved Parliament and ruled the country with the army. In 1658 he died and his son Richard took his place, but he **abdicated** in 1659. General Monk, a soldier who wanted the king back, gathered loyal Royalists and asked Charles II to return. Charles declared that he would pardon everyone except those directly involved in his father's death.

In 1660 he returned and the monarchy was restored.

The new king was welcomed rapturously by huge crowds tired of Cromwell's harsh rule. Charles was called 'the Merrie Monarch', and he cancelled all Cromwell's Acts; in May 1661 a 40-metre-high (130 feet) maypole was erected and people danced happily. But Charles's love of pleasure was balanced by caution. He was determined not to lose the throne, nor to plunge England again into such hardship. He kept quiet about his belief in the Divine Right of Kings and his Catholic sympathies, for the majority of the people were determined to keep Catholics off the English throne. Unfortunately Charles's wife, the Portuguese Catherine of Braganza, bore no children. Charles had fourteen children by his mistresses, but **illegitimate** children could not inherit the throne. The next heir was his Catholic brother James.

OLIVER CROMWELL
1649-1658

The English hated his strict rule, which outlawed entertainment.

The Great Fire of London, 1666
It helped to purify the city after the terrible outbreak of bubonic plague in 1665. It destroyed about 13,000 houses in four days. Charles helped to clean up.

JAMES II
1685-1688 (b. 1633)

The Battle of Sedgemoor, 6 July 1685
James's army completely crushed the Duke of Monmouth's rebellion.

James II

Soon after Charles II's death the Duke of Monmouth, Charles's eldest illegitimate son, was proclaimed king by a group of Protestant rebels. James II, Charles II's brother, defeated the rebels at the Battle of Sedgemoor. Monmouth was executed.

James was wilful and tactless, and believed strongly in the Divine Right of Kings. He dismissed Parliament; cancelled many of the anti-Catholic laws and persecuted Protestants. People were discontented, but they did not want another civil war. So they pinned their hopes on James's heir, his daughter Mary. She was a Protestant, and wife of the Protestant King William of Orange.

THE STUARTS

In 1688, however, James's second wife, the Catholic Mary of Modena (in Italy), had a son. This horrified the English who had not forgotten 'Bloody Mary' (Mary I). They would not accept a line of Catholic rulers, since the Protestant religion was at last securely established. So Parliament invited William of Orange and Mary to rule England. James's men deserted him, and he fled to France.

Judge Jeffreys (known as 'the hanging judge') conducts the 'Bloody Assizes'
This was the trial of Monmouth's supporters after the Battle of Sedgemoor. They were shown no mercy – 320 were executed and over 800 condemned to slavery.

Isaac Newton
Watching a falling apple prompted him to work out the laws of gravity in 1665. His theory of gravity was published in 1685, and his great work on physics, the Principia, in 1687.

THE STUARTS

WILLIAM
1689-1702 (b. 1650)
MARY
1689-1694 (b. 1662)

James Edward Stuart (1688-1766)
He was admired for his intelligence and his good looks. He was brought up at the French court, where in 1701 he was proclaimed King of Great Britain and Ireland. But he never ruled.

William III and Mary II

Mary was James II's daughter, but her baby half-brother was the rightful heir. William was also descended from Charles I, but even further removed from the royal line of descent. Again Parliament had stepped in to stop a king who believed that he had the right to do whatever he liked.

Mary refused to rule without William. William also insisted that he should be king, and not just **Regent.** Parliament had to accept this. Even so, it was clear that Parliament was now more powerful than the monarch.

The Bank of England
It was founded in 1694 to do the government's financial business

They made certain of this by issuing two **declarations**: monarchs would not be allowed either to make or cancel laws, or have an army, without Parliament's consent; and Parliament had to be summoned to meet regularly.

In 1690 James, with Irish support, tried to regain his crown. William's forces defeated him at the Battle of the Boyne. Mary took little part in politics. She was a devoted wife, and William was heartbroken when she died of smallpox in 1694.

The Catholic countries of Europe did not like England's Protestantism, nor did they like the loss of royal power and the breaking of the laws of succession, for it set a dangerous example. The Catholic Church and its European monarchs wanted to hold on to their power. France made war on England, trying to restore James as king. When James died in 1701, King Louis XIV of France called James's son, James Edward, 'King of Great Britain and Ireland'. Meanwhile, William's lack of charm and his increasing brutality towards Catholics made him unpopular in England. He was not much mourned after his death in a riding accident.

The Massacre of Glencoe

The Scots supported the exiled James II but William made them swear loyalty to him and Mary. The MacDonalds of Glencoe took the oath a few days late. In revenge, William asked their ancient enemies, the Campbells, to kill all of the Macdonalds. The Campbells accepted the MacDonalds' hospitality, then on 13 February 1692 they murdered thirty-eight of them. After the Scots realised William had ordered this, they never trusted him again.

THE STUARTS

ANNE
1702-1714 (b. 1665)

In 1709 Daniel Defoe wrote Robinson Crusoe, based on the real adventures of the Scottish sailor Alexander Selkirk, rescued that year from a desert island where he had lived for four years.

Anne

Anne took more interest in drinking tea (a new fashion) and betting on horse races than in affairs of state. John Churchill, the husband of Anne's favourite, Sarah, became one of the finest and most renowned of English generals. Under him, the British army and its allies kept Spain from taking over most of Europe, and ended France's support of the Stuart claim to the English throne.

Even so, Anne's life was troubled because of problems connected with the succession. She had joined other Protestants in offering the throne to William and Mary, but she never forgave herself for betraying her father, James II. She believed that her ill health and the loss of seventeen children either during pregnancy or in their early childhood was punishment for this.

As she was left childless, another heir had to be chosen. James's Catholic son would never be allowed to reign, but Anne and her advisers did not like the alternative. This was the ruling house of Hanover in Germany. Its members were descended from Charles I's sister Elizabeth, who had married the King of Bohemia.

A German monarch would not be welcome. On the other hand, James II's son, James Edward Stuart, would not give up his Catholic faith. There were no more surviving descendants of Charles I, so eventually the Hanoverians were invited to take the throne.

Queen Anne loved watching the horses at the races.

GEORGE I
1714-1727 (b. 1660)

Weaving tools and machinery

Improvements in these during George's reign increased production. This was the start of the 'Industrial Revolution' which transformed British life in the 18th and 19th centuries.

George I

At Anne's death the crown went to George, Elector (ruler) of Hanover in Germany. George did not like England, and he knew that the English did not really want him as their king, but had chosen his family just to keep the Catholic Stuarts out. He preferred Hanover, his home, where he had absolute power.

George hated painting and poetry. He did enjoy music, and brought the great composer Handel to England. But George rarely visited England and never learnt English. In 1721 one of the government **ministers** was given the job of speaking for the king in meetings. This man, Robert Walpole, was called the 'prime' (meaning 'chief') minister.

Because George had so little interest in governing England, the **monarchy** had even less power by the end of his reign.

His eldest son was also called George. The two hated each other, for the son had never forgiven his father for divorcing his mother.

George II

As king, George II resembled George I, the father he had hated so much. He even hated *his* eldest son, Frederick. British military success continued. In 1743 George himself led his troops to victory against France at the Battle of Dettingen. During the Seven Years War (1756-63) when Britain and Prussia (part of what is now Germany) fought France to gain **colonies** in India and America, William Pitt became a great military leader. By 1759 Britain ruled the seas, and owned most of Canada, India, and the West Indies.

When Frederick died in 1751, his son, another George, became George II's successor.

GEORGE II
1727-1760 (b. 1683)

**1752
SEPTEMBER**
1 2 (14) 15 16 17
18 19 20 21 22 23 2
25 26 27

In 1752 the Gregorian calendar was adopted.

It was twelve days ahead of the old (Julian) calendar, so the day after 2 September was 14 September. People rioted, believing their lives had been shortened.

'Bonnie Prince Charlie' (Charles, Son of James Edward Stuart), the 'Young Pretender', escapes after the failure of his attempt in 1745 to gain the throne. This was the second 'Jacobite rebellion'.

GEORGE III
1760-1820 (b. 1738)

George III

George III was the first Hanoverian king to be born in Britain. He was known as 'Farmer George' because of his interest in agriculture. He regained some of the power lost by George I, but he did not keep it.

Britain was now a very powerful nation, owning many colonies – but guarding them was costly. The American colonists protested at the heavy taxes that Britain made them pay, and in 1770 all American taxes were abolished except the tax on tea. This was kept so that Britain would not lose the right to tax Americans. Boston, in Massachusetts, rebelled against the tea tax, so Britain took away Boston's rights as a colony. This angered all Americans, and in 1775 the War of Independence (now called the American Revolution) began between Britain and America. In 1783, after Britain's surrender, American independence was officially recognised.

The Boston Tea Party

In 1770 British troops shot dead five anti-tax protesters in Boston, Massachusetts. In 1773 a group of angry Bostonians dressed up as American Indians and tipped British tea cargoes into the sea.

Britain was more successful in the other great conflict of George's reign. Two great leaders, Lord Horatio Nelson at sea, and the Duke of Wellington on land, defeated Napoleon, **dictatorial** Emperor of the newly formed French **Republic**, in **campaigns** conducted between 1793 and 1815.

At home, the Industrial Revolution was at its peak and Britain's wealth steadily increased. A group called the Luddites rioted, and smashed machinery, fearing that it would take jobs away from working people. They were proved right in 1816. After the expense of the war in Europe, other countries could no longer afford to buy British goods. Jobs were lost, and poverty ruled.

By this time George no longer held power. He had shown signs of madness in 1788. By 1811 he was quite mad and his son George was Prince Regent, acting for the king.

The Battle of Waterloo, 18 June 1815

The British and Prussian armies under Wellington and General Blücher overcame Napoleon's French forces.

Lord Nelson, at the Battle of Copenhagen in 1801, puts his telescope to his blind eye, so as to ignore a command to retreat.

THE HANOVERIANS

GEORGE IV
1820-1830 (b. 1762)

Brighton Pavilion, designed for George by the architect John Nash

Nash's buildings can also be seen in Bath and Regent's Park, London. Their style is still imitated today.

George IV

George IV had been a stylish Prince of Wales, but his wild behaviour brought disgrace to the monarchy. The country was poor after the expense of the wars against Napoleon, and unemployment was high. George was soon hated for his lavish spending, and for treating his wife, whom he disliked, very badly. He had been forced to marry her, and he did not find her at all attractive. He tried to divorce her, but she died in 1821. George was so pigheaded and selfish that the **Whigs**, who were not then in power, agreed that when they had the chance they would remove all remaining royal power.

George's one good point was that he loved and encouraged the arts and architecture. The beautiful 'Regency' style of architecture was named after him, because it emerged with George's encouragement when he was Prince Regent (1811-20).

William IV

William IV, George's younger brother, was known as 'the Sailor King', because he had been a sailor from the age of thirteen. He hated ceremony, and his sensible behaviour was a refreshing change. He tried to hold on to what little power the **sovereign** still had, and opposed the Reform **Bills** of 1831 and 1832, which aimed to take away that power. When rioting followed the blocking of the third Reform Bill, William gave in, losing the last remnants of power.

WILLIAM IV
1830-1837 (b. 1765)

The movement towards greater security for workers grew. Trade unions were established to stand up for workers' rights. The Chartist Movement demanded votes for all men. Slavery was abolished in British colonies. Now workers had to be paid to do the work the slaves had been forced to do. The new Poor Law of 1834 provided 'workhouses' to give shelter to the penniless. For them, with no **Welfare State**, unemployment could mean starvation.

Tolpuddle martyrs
In 1834 a group of farm labourers, known as the Tolpuddle martyrs, were transported to Australia for forming a trade union.

A horse-drawn London bus

THE HANOVERIANS

VICTORIA
1837-1901 (b. 1819)

In 1854 Britain and France took Turkey's side in a war against Russia; this became known as the Crimean War (it was fought in the Russian territory called the Crimea). Other European countries later entered the war on the British side. British forces suffered severely from lack of planning; and in the disastrous 'Charge of the Light Brigade' a mistaken order sent almost 700 men of the Light Brigade into a narrow valley, facing a battery of Russian guns. A third of them were killed.

THE HANOVERIANS

Victoria

After William IV's death the crown passed to his young niece, Victoria. The new queen was only eighteen and had led a sheltered life. At her **accession**, Hanover and Britain ceased to be ruled together, because the laws of succession in Hanover barred a woman from ruling.

Victoria had a natural authority, but she quickly became dependent on the Prime Minister, Lord Melbourne, adopting all his opinions. As his attitudes were old-fashioned and strict, Victoria quickly became very unpopular.

In 1840 she married her cousin, Prince Albert of Saxe-Coburg-Gotha (in Germany), and things changed. Albert was not outgoing, and was never much liked by the British people.

However, Victoria adored him and Albert's influence on her, and so on British life, was enormous. Fortunately, Albert was kindhearted, peace-loving, and in many ways open-minded. Family values and strict morality were very important. Albert was given the title 'Prince **Consort**' in 1857, but died of typhoid four years later. On his deathbed he wrote a letter to the president of America, Abraham Lincoln, in connection with a crisis that had flared up between Britain and America. The careful wording of the letter prevented the outbreak of war between the two countries. At the same time, Albert was concerned about the behaviour of Edward, the heir to the throne.

Florence Nightingale, 'the Lady with the Lamp'

She became famous for the quality of nursing care she provided in the Crimea. She and her team of nurses brought the death rate for injured soldiers down from 42% to 2%.

The Crystal Palace

Prince Albert had this built to house his brainchild, the Great Exhibition of 1851. The Crystal Palace was designed by Joseph Paxton and made of glass on an iron frame.

THE HANOVERIANS

VICTORIA
1837-1901 (b. 1819)

Disraeli (right) and Gladstone (left) in the House of Commons

Disraeli was a Conservative. Gladstone, whom Victoria disliked, was a Liberal. They were fierce opponents and held office as Prime Minister alternately in Victoria's reign.

Victoria was devastated by her husband Albert's death. She blamed their son Edward for causing it by his wild behaviour and never forgave him. She wore black, in mourning, for the rest of her life, and made no public appearances for over twenty years.

Her popularity crashed, and there was even talk of abolishing the monarchy, but in 1887 she returned to public life, and her Diamond **Jubilee** in 1897 was a time of great celebration. Since Albert's death Victoria had relied mainly on a Scottish servant, John Brown. She remained very close to him, despite public disapproval. She also very much liked Benjamin Disraeli, prime minister from 1874 to 1880. Disraeli made her Empress of India in 1876, and she was grief-stricken at his death in 1881.

Victoria's reign was coloured by her strong feelings, and most of all, her deep grief at the loss of Albert.

She was strong-willed as well and her personality and beliefs affected national life. She believed in strict morality. She really cared about working people, believing that they were the heart of Britain. Her reign saw the limiting of the working day to ten hours, the introduction of basic education for all, and other measures aimed at improving the living conditions of the poor.

Victoria lived so long, and had so many children, that she was eventually a senior figure in all the royal families of Europe. This brought her considerable influence and authority. She was even called 'the grandmother of Europe'. This was one of the reasons why, after the Crimean War, her reign saw a long period of peace in Europe.

By the time Victoria died in 1901, Britain was the most powerful nation in the world, at the head of a vast empire, and with influence in the rest of Europe.

British settlers riding on an Indian elephant
British territory in India had been growing since 1600.

THE HANOVERIANS

EDWARD VII
1901-1910 (b. 1841)

Edward laughed so much at a Royal Command Performance of a play by George Bernard Shaw that he broke his chair.

The first Boy Scout camp
This took place on Brownsea Island, Dorset, in 1907.

Edward VII

Victoria's son Edward had been very strictly brought up, and both his parents had disliked him. In spite of all this, he was a kind man, although he had the hot temper of the Hanoverians. He was popular, for he was deeply concerned about the conditions of the poor, and the gap between rich and poor.

Society was changing rapidly. In 1906 Emmeline Pankhurst started the **Suffragette Movement**, demanding that women be given the right to vote in parliamentary elections.

Edward earned the title 'the Peacemaker' because of his efforts to bring about good relations with other countries. He also foresaw the possibility that Germany, a nation greedy for power, might cause a major war. His death occurred in the middle of a crisis, after the House of Lords rejected a Liberal budget aimed at helping the poor.

George V

Edward's son, George V, was a sailor like William IV. He was shy, and he disliked ceremony. He took his duties very seriously. In 1917 he gave up his family name of Saxe-Coburg-Gotha and took the surname 'Windsor', after Windsor Castle. He did this because his original name was German, and Britain and Germany were at war.

In the 1930s most of the population became poverty-stricken in the economic crisis known as the 'Great Depression'.

GEORGE V
1910-1936 (b. 1865)

In 1913 suffragette Emily Davidson threw herself in front of George's horse in the Derby

George was very concerned and went to meet people who were suffering hardship. He also gave up part of his own income.

In 1935 George was genuinely surprised at the extent of the celebrations for his Silver Jubilee. He had not realised he was so popular and that people liked him. He died peacefully the year after. He was one of the very few monarchs in Europe who had kept his throne after the First World War.

In 1919 the **Irish Republican Army** *(IRA) was founded to free Ireland from British rule.*

GEORGE VI
1936-1952 (b. 1895)

EDWARD VIII
Jan-Dec 1936 (b. 1894)

Edward and his wife-to-be, Wallis Simpson
After their marriage they were known as the Duke and Duchess of Windsor.

George VI

George V's eldest son, Edward, was a popular Prince of Wales. He was charming and handsome and cared about poor people. He was brave, too, and had wanted to fight in the First World War.

Unfortunately, at the time of George's death, Edward was in love with a married woman, the American Mrs Simpson. In October 1936 she and her husband divorced, and Edward seemed set on marrying her. This was impossible, as he was now head of the Church of England, and the Church did not approve of divorce. This royal marriage drama overshadowed important issues such as unemployment, the civil war in Spain, and the rise to power, in Germany, of Adolf Hitler. In December 1936, Edward abdicated and his brother, the Duke of York, became George VI.

George VI was a shy, frail man with a stammer. He found kingship difficult. His wife, Elizabeth, was his biggest asset. During the Second World War (1939-45) Adolf Hitler, the German leader, called her 'the most dangerous woman in Europe'. This was because her courage and cheerfulness inspired and comforted the whole nation. When bombing started, she was asked to take her two daughters to safety in Canada. She refused. Even when Buckingham Palace was bombed, she remained cheerful, saying, 'Now I can look the East End in the face.' (The East End of London had been bombed shortly before.) The couple and their daughters, Elizabeth and Margaret, presented a picture of contented and dutiful family life, giving a sense of security to a nation at war.

Gandhi

He led the peaceful movement for Indian independence. In 1947 years of struggle in India ended with independence for India and Pakistan. During George's reign many other colonies became independent, with Britain's encouragement.

George and Elizabeth visited London's East End after it was bombed during the Second World War.

ELIZABETH II
1952- (b. 1926)

Elizabeth has strived to keep the image of the royal family modern and relevant throughout her reign. In 1953, when she was crowned, television was still a novelty. Elizabeth insisted, against the advice of Prime Minister Winston Churchill and the Archbishop of Canterbury, that her coronation ceremony should be televised.

Elizabeth II

Under Elizabeth, the role of the monarch has changed in many ways. Today, the Queen is largely symbolic, having no real political power. But she makes the most of her position by acting as an **ambassador** of good will for the British government at home and overseas. She has always shown a sense of duty, common sense and concern for her subjects, including those in the **Commonwealth**.

Elizabeth's reign has seen a dramatic growth in global communication through television and, more recently, the internet. From televising the Queen's coronation in 1953 to today's interviews and official websites, the royal family has moved with the times to maintain a positive and open relationship with the public through the media.

Attitudes to women and marriage have changed enormously since the Second World War. The Queen's husband, Prince Philip, has supported her in many of her official roles and helped her to bear her responsibilities.

Increased media coverage of Elizabeth's family and business affairs means it is now much easier to criticize the monarchy than ever before. Many say that the royal family is unnecessary, old-fashioned and expensive. In response, the Queen chose to pay taxes, found ways to cut royal costs and opened Buckingham Palace to the public. Today you can even find the royal family's business accounts online!

The British monarchy has had to evolve with changes in society and politics since the time of William I. Elizabeth's intelligent reign has built upon that tradition and helped today's royal family to remain popular and find a place in the modern world.

Charles, Prince of Wales, and his wife Diana on their wedding day in 1981

The international media followed the lives of the Prince and Princess of Wales through marriage, separation and divorce, often making headline news. In 1997 Diana died in a car crash in Paris along with companion Dodi Al Fayed.

Prince Charles was married again in 2005, to his long-term friend Camilla Parker Bowles.

THE WINDSORS

Glossary

abdicate to give up being monarch

accession when the heir to the throne becomes ruler

ambassador someone who represents his or her country abroad

Anglo-Saxon a Saxon who inhabited England before the Norman Conquest or the language spoken by Anglo-Saxons

aristocracy the group of people in society with titles such as, 'Earl' or 'Duchess'. People of high rank

assizes courts of law, usually holding regular sessions

Bill a proposed law which has not yet been approved by the monarch or by Parliament

campaign a series of military actions aimed at a particular result

colony a territory taken and governed by one country, located in another country; a colonist is a settler there

Commonwealth the group of nations which were once ruled by Britain, and now govern themselves

consort the husband or wife of a monarch

counterfeiter a person who forges coins. Severe punishments were handed out to these criminals

Covenant an agreement made in 1638 to protect some Scots' special form of Protestant worship. It was entered into in 1643 by English Parliamentarians

Crusades a series of 'Holy Wars' waged by European Christians on Muslims in the 11th-13th centuries, in an attempt to win Jerusalem, the 'holy city' of both religions

Danegeld payments by Saxon rulers to the Vikings to stop them attacking. From 991 rulers raised these payments by taxation. The Norman kings continued to make people pay this tax until 1162

Danelaw the part of England controlled by the Vikings

decimal a counting system based on the number ten

declaration an official announcement

depose to force a monarch from the throne

devout deeply and faithfully religious

dictatorial exercising power selfishly and cruelly

Divine Right of Kings the belief that a monarch by birth rules by God's will rather than by the people's will

dynasty a ruling family, in which power is passed down by inheritance

earl in Saxon times, a ruler of one of the English 'kingdoms', owing loyalty to the king. As the king's power increased, the power of the earls decreased a little, although they, like other nobles, could and did cause trouble for unpopular kings

El Dorado (means 'the golden one' in Spanish) a mythical country full of gold

excommunicate to expel someone from membership of the Christian Church and ban them from attending services

famine a period of mass starvation, usually resulting from a failure of the usual food supply

feudal society the division of society into classes. Each class worked for the class above in exchange for land and protection

freeman in feudal society, a free man with legal rights. That is, a member of any class but the lowest

frontier the border of a country or territory

heir the person, usually the monarch's eldest son, who has the right to inherit the throne

Holy Roman Emperor the ruler of the Holy (that is, Christian) Roman Empire, which covered a large area of Europe

hostage in war, someone given into enemy hands as a guarantee that the hostage-givers will keep an agreement.

House of Commons the British House of Parliament whose members are chosen by vote, and who have most of the power in government

House of Lords the British House of Parliament whose members are not elected by the public

Hundred Years War a series of battles between England and France fought during the years from 1337 to 1453, chiefly over parts of France claimed by the English

illegitimate born to parents who were not legally married and therefore not entitled to inherit wealth, rank, or property from the father

invalid not legally acceptable

Irish Republican Army (IRA) a group set up in 1919 to fight for Irish independence from Britain, and union between Northern and Southern Ireland

Jubilee an anniversary, especially of a monarch's coronation

last rites the Christian ritual for a person about to die

massacre the killing of a large number of virtually defenceless people at one time

minister a person whose job is to take part in government

monarch a king or queen

monarchy government under a king or queen

New Model Army the well-trained army created in 1645 by Oliver Cromwell during the English Civil War

Parliamentarians the people who supported Parliament against the king in the English Civil War

peer (in this book) a nobleman. It can also mean 'an equal'

penance punishment for a sin against religious principles

persecute to abuse and mistreat someone, especially because of his or her nationality or religion

plunder to rob or steal greedily, especially in war

poll tax a tax payable by every person ('poll' is an old word for 'head', especially used to refer to 'counting heads')

Puritans a group of Protestants who thought that all pleasure and enjoyment was a sin

ravage to damage, plunder and terrorise (a country or region)

Regent someone appointed to rule for a monarch who is too young, or ill, or absent

Renaissance the flowering of art and learning which took place, starting in Italy, during the 14th to 17th centuries

Republic a self-governing country ruled by an elected president, not a monarch

revenue profit or financial gain from one particular source

scutage 'shield tax' that knights and barons had to pay if they did not fight in the king's army

serf (or villein) a member of the lowest class in feudal society. Serfs were forced to work for their lords, had no legal rights, and could not own land

sovereign a monarch

Suffragette Movement a campaign in the early 20th century fighting for women's right to vote

trade union an organised group of workers in a particular trade, formed to protect the rights of all workers in that trade

treaty a written agreement, usually between countries that have been at war

treason the crime of betraying the monarch or the nation

Wars of the Roses the name given in the 19th century to the thirty-year (1455-85) struggle for the crown between the houses of Lancaster and York

Welfare State the system established in the 1940s to protect the poor; providing housing, an income, and health care

Wessex the ancient West Saxon kingdom, covering most of southwest England. It was the heart of Anglo-Saxon England

Whigs the British political party in the 17th to 19th centuries that opposed the monarchy

Index

To download a free timeline showing the kings and queens of England, go to: www.ladybird.com/kingsandqueens

A catalogue record for this book is available from the British Library

Published by Ladybird Books Ltd
A Penguin Company
Penguin Books Ltd., 80 Strand, London WC2R 0RL, UK
Penguin Books Australia Ltd., Camberwell, Victoria, Australia
Penguin Group (NZ) 67 Apollo Drive, Rosedale, North Shore 0632, New Zealand

002 – 2 3 4 5 6 7 8 9 10
© Ladybird Books Limited MCMXCVI
This edition MMXI

ISBN: 978-1-40930-873-7

Printed in China